The Guide to
WOODEN
BOATS

The Guide to
WOODEN BOATS

SCHOONERS
KETCHES
CUTTERS
SLOOPS
YAWLS
CATS

Photographs by Benjamin Mendlowitz
Text by Maynard Bray
Foreword by Joel White

W.W. Norton & Company
New York • London

Other books of photography by Benjamin Mendlowitz:
Wood, Water & Light
A Passage in Time,
The Book of Wooden Boats

Text copyright ©1997 by Maynard Bray
Photographs copyright © 1997 by Benjamin Mendlowitz
Design by Sherry Streeter, Brooklin, Maine
Illustrations by Kathy Bray
Production by NOAH Publications, Brooklin, Maine

Printed by Tien Wah Press, Singapore.
First edition

Library of Congress Cataloging-in-Publication Data
    The guide to wooden boats : schooners, ketches, cutters, sloops, yawls,
cats / photographs by Benjamin Mendlowitz : text by Maynard Bray
            p.   cm.
    Includes index.
    ISBN 0-393-04045-3
    1. Sailboats. 2. Wooden boats. I. Bray, Maynard. II. Title.

VM351.M44 1996
623.8'203--dc20   96-23419

W. W. Norton & Company, Inc., 500 Fifth Avenue, New York, N.Y. 10110
W. W. Norton & Company Ltd. 10 Coptic Street, London WC1A 1PU
http: web.wwnorton.com

1 2 3 4 5 6 7 8 9 0

PHOTO ™ This mark of assurance certifies that the
VERITÉ photographs in this book are accurate
reproductions of what the camera
recorded. The publisher guarantees that they have not been altered
in any way, either through digital manipulation or photo combination. This mark can only be used by publishers and photographers
who have made authenticity guarantees through the Photo Verite
license agreement. For further information please inquire at NOAH
Publications 207-359-9895.

This book is dedicated to our wives, Deborah and Anne, without whose support this book couldn't possibly exist. We also wish to thank designer Sherry Streeter, editor James Mairs, and Joel White, Kathy Bray, Stephen Corkery, and Claire Cramer, who all worked with us on this book. Our appreciation extends to the countless boat designers, boatbuilders, boat owners, and sailors through whose efforts these beautiful craft are created, restored, and maintained.

Contents

Foreword

This book, though small in size, is large in content. There are pictures and text covering 136 boats of all sizes, types, and rigs. The selection of boats is subdivided by rig, so that the reader can compare, for instance, a Friendship sloop with a skipjack sloop, or a husky Baltic trader ketch with the sleek Herreshoff ketch *Ticonderoga*.

The credentials of the authors are impeccable. Benjamin Mendlowitz is world-renowned as a marine photographer, specializing in images of wooden boats looking their best. His photography is invariably appealing, for the boat is always shown from the most favorable angle; the lighting is strong or even dramatic, and the background attractive without being intrusive. What is even more remarkable about these pictures is their reality. In these times of digitization and computer enhancement of images, Ben's photos are without tricks. What you see is what the photographer saw as his shutter opened. The sky is the real sky, not one plucked from a computer memory. The image appears as Ben composed it, free from the distractions of unsightly dinghies, bizarrely dressed crew members, or unfortunate background objects.

To achieve this degree of realism means spending countless hours waiting for the moment, trailing one's prey as a lion tracks an antelope. I have observed Ben doing this—in the early morning, when the light is low and strong; in a brisk midafternoon sou'wester, when the air is full of spray and sunlight; or in the evening when the wind is down, the sun is sinking, and amazing colors flare in the sky. His patience is relentless, the perfect image always in his mind.

Just as Ben seeks the boat's essence with his photographs, Maynard Bray strives to convey the boat's personality with his brief captions accompanying each picture. I know of no other person whose knowledge of wooden boats is so encyclopaedic, inquisitive, and admiring. While the space limits of this book prevent Maynard from informing us at length about each boat (much as he would like to), even these thumbnail sketches go to the core of the subject. Like Ben's images, Maynard's prose descriptions of the boats are concise and accurate.

During a photographic session, Maynard often drives the chase boat for Ben. His skill at setting up shots is instinctive, and few words pass between photographer and driver. It is a lesson in symbiotic relationships to watch them at work.

For those interested in the beauty, romance, and craftsmanship of wooden boats, this book will bring an awareness of the diversity of the resource, a catalog of the treasures that still grace our waterways. If it inspires some to participate in the preservation of these treasures, it is all the more worthwhile.

Joel White
Brooklin, Maine

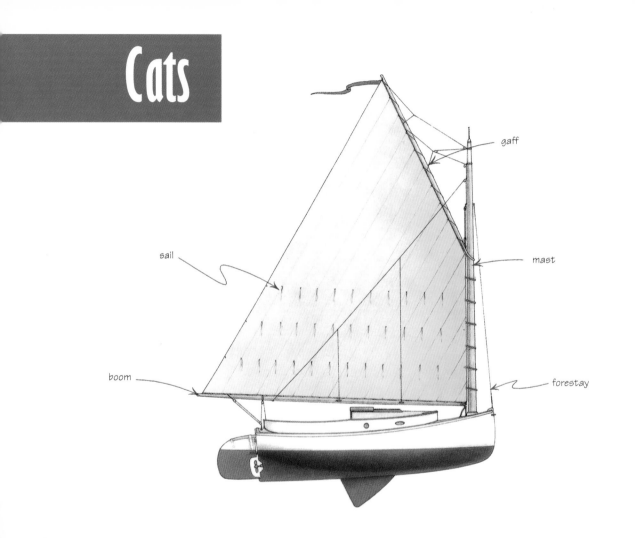

Cats

gaff

sail

mast

boom

forestay

Boats rigged as cats have a single mast and only one sail. This is the simplest possible rig, and sailing a small boat with a cat rig is easier as well. Cat rigs are found in the smallest open sailing dinghies, such as the Nutshell prams (page 17) and also in boats that are big enough to cruise in. In most cases, you'll see either three-sided marconi sails or four-sided gaff sails, but there are other variations, such as lug, sprit, and lateen sails. The mast of many cat-rigged boats is stepped near the bow where there's not enough beam to make shrouds practical, so in such instances a stouter mast that can stand on its own is necessary.

If a sail is too big, it becomes difficult for the usual one- or two-person crew to raise, trim, reef, or furl. Boats above, say, 25 feet usually abandon the cat rig and distribute the sail area among two or more sails, thus avoiding a single, enormous mainsail.

Among the cat-rigged boat types, catboats come first to mind. To qualify as a catboat (as opposed to a cat-rigged boat), the hull as well as the rig must conform: Catboats have shallow hulls that are almost half as wide as they are long and, in general, originated near Cape Cod, Massachusetts, Eastern Long Island, or the Barnegat Bay area of New Jersey. While there are exceptions, catboats generally have centerboards and decks, and rudders that are long and no deeper than the hull itself.

Cimba

25'0" x 11'8" Cape Cod catboat • Designed by Fenwick C. Williams • Built by Herbert Baum • Kennebunkport, ME • 1965

A BLUSTERY WIND CALLS FOR REEFING. With only a little more than half her sail area spread, *Cimba* scoots before the snapping nor'wester under perfect control. Catboats this big have wheels instead of tillers to make steering easier; even with a deep reef, *Cimba* wants to round up into the wind because of the weather helm that is typical of the cat rig.

Conjurer

27'0" x 12'0" Cape Cod catboat • Designed and built by H. Manley Crosby • Osterville, Massachusetts • 1909

CAPE COD CATBOATS ARE NEARLY HALF AS WIDE AS THEY ARE LONG, and as a result, have wonderfully roomy cockpits—and cabins, too, except for headroom. Shallow draft is another virtue: With her centerboard raised, *Conjurer* needs only a couple of feet of water, just the thing for roaming the shoals south of the Cape.

Breck Marshall

20'0" x 9'8" Cape Cod catboat • Designed by Charles Crosby • Built by Mystic Seaport Museum • Mystic, CT • 1987

THE BIG COCKPIT AND SHALLOW DRAFT MAKE THIS CATBOAT IDEAL FOR CARRYING PASSENGERS, six at a time, along the waterfront of Mystic Seaport Museum. Faithful to her tradition, she's fitted with manila running rigging and a cotton sail, which, in this late afternoon light, takes on a rich glow that befits a natural material.

Peggotty

17'6" x 9'0" • Built by Robert H. Baker • Westport, Massachusetts • 1977

NOT ALL CATBOATS HAVE CENTERBOARDS. *Peggotty*'s shallow keel, while not as effective in preventing leeway, enables some degree of windward work. A single halyard hoists the sail—an unusual arrangement (most gaff sails have two, a peak and a throat halyard), but workable here because the gaff is short and not highly peaked.

Beetle Cat

12'0" x 6'0" • Designed by John Beetle • Built by Concordia Co. • South Dartmouth, Massachusetts • Since 1948

HEAVIER BOATS CAN CARRY MORE SAIL, all else being equal, and for her length, a Beetle Cat is heavy. She's decked and has floorboards and inner planking called ceiling, all of which add weight compared to an open sailing dinghy. The Beetle Cat's weight, combined with her generous beam, allows a big sail, which speeds the boat along in light air.

Josef W.

15'3" x 3'9" Delaware ducker • Designed by Josef Liener • Built by The Rockport Apprentice Shop • Rockport, ME • 1978

THESE BOATS HAVE TWO RIGS, one large for racing and the other small for everyday use. Duckers are decked double-enders that can be either rowed or sailed, and poled when roaming through the marsh grass after railbirds. The ducker's boom is higher than the Beetle Cat's because the helmsman sits higher up in the boat.

Finch

11'2" x 4'5" Shellback dinghy • Designed by Joel White • Built by Mark Littlehales • Brooklin, Maine • 1989

IT ONLY TAKES ONE HALYARD to hoist a lugsail, but the halyard has to be tied to the yard in exactly the right place—as determined by trial and error—or else the sail won't set well. A chief advantage of a rig like this is that all the spars are short enough to fit inside the boat.

Nutshell Prams

7'7" x 4'0" • Designed by Joel White • Built by various builders since 1983

NUTSHELLS ARE VERSATILE: You can row them, sail them, or tow them as a tender to a larger boat. A single 'midship frame is all that's needed, because they're planked with strakes of plywood whose edges are lapped and glued to each other. And because plywood doesn't shrink, these prams (as well as the Shellbacks) don't leak when first launched after being ashore.

Silent Maid

33'0" x 12'6" • Barnegat Bay catboat • Designed by Francis Sweisguth • Built by Morton Johnson & Co. • Bay Head, NJ • 1924

MARCONI-RIGGED CATBOATS OF 1920S ORIGIN STILL RACE ON BARNEGAT BAY'S PROTECTED WATERS. Their tall masts require shrouds and backstays, in addition to the headstay, to keep them standing. Reducing the spread of sail by reefing, of course, is another way of preventing a dismasting or a capsize. The challenge here is deciding which of the five reefs to tie in when it breezes up.

Mary Ann

28'2" x 10'10" Barnegat Bay A-Cat · Designed by Charles D. Mower · Built by Benjamin River Marine · Brooklin, ME · 1988

A LIGHT-AIR FLYER WITH HER BIG SAIL, you'd best take heed when the wind picks up. When she heels enough to submerge the leeward deck, it's time to reef—or at least spill some wind by luffing. Because there's no outside ballast keel, there's a limit to how far boats like this can be heeled without losing their stability and going all the way over in a capsize.

Andros Dinghy

13'0" x 4'2" • Modeled and built by Bernard Longley • Lisbon Creek, Mangrove Cay, Bahamas • 1977

THESE KIDS ARE NATURAL SEAMEN because being on the water is so much a part of their lives. They're ready to slack the sheet if hit by an overpowering puff, and a hiking board allows one boy to shift his weight further to windward. A sculling oar is always at the ready to be used in the transom-mounted sculling notch if auxiliary power is needed.

Windrose and *Hesperus*

14'6" x 5'0" Abaco dinghies • Modeled and built by Joseph Albury • Man-O-War Cay, Bahamas • 1989

MOST SAILING DINGHIES HAVE CAT RIGS, and, even with this simplest of rigs, there's plenty to do. One hand is always on the tiller, and the other holds the sheet—especially if it's blowing like this. Your weight, located on the windward rail, acts as ballast to prevent a capsize, but that's not likely to be enough in a sudden puff. Then it's time to quickly slack the sheet, which is why it's not cleated.

Sloops

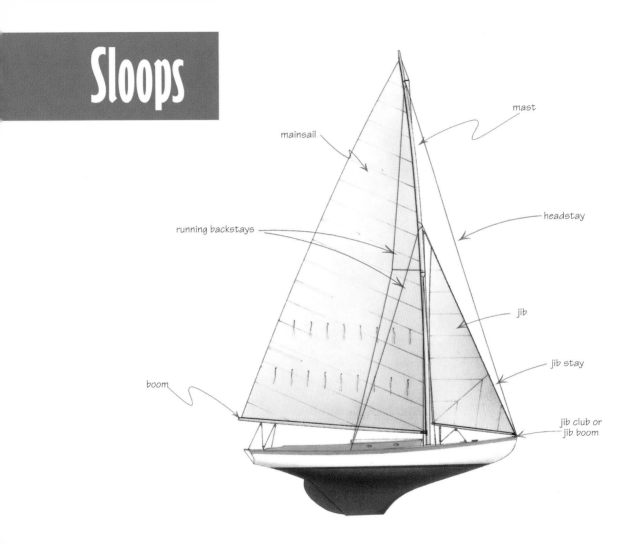

mast

mainsail

headstay

running backstays

jib

jib stay

boom

jib club or
jib boom

Sloops come in all sizes—some more than 100 feet long—and can be recognized by *a single mast, a single mainsail, and, generally, a single jib.* These days there's a gray area between sloop and cutter: Refer to the cutter chapter introduction on page 59 for more detail in this regard. The sloop rig is, by far, the most popular of all rigs in this country today. There's good reason for this. First, for a given sail area, a sloop is noticeably faster than a cat; second, aside from a cat, it is the least complicated and least costly to produce and maintain; and, finally, a sloop is easier to learn to sail than the other rigs, with the exception of the cat.

There is more to sailing a sloop than a cat, not only because a sloop is likely to be larger, but due to there being an additional halyard and sheet for hoisting and trimming the jib. Some sloops, especially larger ones designed for racing, have big, overlapping jibs known as genoas. And for downwind sailing, a sloop, when racing, usually sets a parachutelike sail called a spinnaker. (Spinnakers are also seen on cutters and yawls, and, to a lesser extent, on ketches and schooners.)

Masts for sloops are stepped farther aft than in a cat so there's space forward for the jib. And as with cats, sloops can be rigged with gaff or marconi mainsails, or one of the more rare gunter or lug sails. It makes no difference whether the forestay goes partway up the mast (fractional rig) or all the way (as in a masthead rig), or if there's a bowsprit, a boomkin, or even a boom; if she meets the above criteria, she's a sloop.

Freda

33'0" x 12'2" • Modeled & built by Harry Cookson • Belvedere, California • 1885

HUNDREDS OF GAFF SLOOPS LIKE *FREDA* ONCE SAILED SAN FRANCISCO WATERS. First made obsolete by engine-driven boats, then by automobiles and trucks, sailing craft like *Freda* generally met their end not long after the turn of the century. It's nearly unheard-of today for a boat still sailing to have been launched only a generation after the California Gold Rush.

Puffin

18'0" x 8'0" sandbagger sloop • Designed by A. Cary Smith • Built by The Rockport Apprentice Shop • Rockport, ME • 1990

OVERCANVASED FOR THE SPORT OF IT, sandbagger sloops like *Puffin* always give their crews plenty of excitement; just avoiding a capsize when the wind breezes up calls for large measures of coordination and judgment. In their heyday, more than a century ago, racing sandbaggers was like horse racing in that observers bet money on the outcome and professionals did the racing.

Eastward

32'1" x 10'6" Friendship sloop • Designed by Murray G. Peterson • Built by James Chadwick • Pemaquid, Maine • 1956

LONG A FAMILIAR SIGHT ON THE MAINE COAST, *Eastward* has always been owned by Roger and Mary Duncan, who have built their summertime lives around her, researching for *The Cruising Guide to the New England Coast,* teaching seamanship, racing other Friendships, and day chartering near home at Boothbay Harbor. To witness first-class boat handling, fair weather or foul, just follow *Eastward* and keep your eyes open.

Amity

30'3" x 10'0" Friendship sloop • Modeled & built by Wilbur A. Morse • Friendship, Maine • 1901

FRIENDSHIP SLOOPS WERE THE LOBSTERBOATS OF THE LATE 19TH CENTURY. In those days of commercial sail it took a steady, maneuverable craft with a good turn of speed to satisfy a lobsterman, and along the mid-Maine coast these handsome sloops became the boats of choice. But when gasoline-powered boats came into use many Friendships were abandoned while others, like *Amity*, were converted for pleasure.

Amorita

43'6" x 8'9" New York 30 • Designed by N.G. Herreshoff • Built by Herreshoff Mfg. Co. • Bristol, Rhode Island • 1905

ONE OF THE BEST-LOVED WOODEN ONE-DESIGN CLASSES is the New York 30, of which 18 were built during a single winter. Considered day boats for 'round-the-buoy racing when new, they later gained stature as cruisers as the sport of yachting changed over the years. Because of their adaptability and in spite of their age, about half of the original fleet is still sailing.

Naiad

32'0" x 9'3" Buzzards Bay 25 • Designed by N.G. Herreshoff • Built by Concordia Co. • So. Dartmouth, MA • 1983

ONE OF THE ALL-TIME BEAUTIES surely is this design. Five came out of the Herreshoff yard in 1914, but lately others, including *Naiad*, have been launched. While most of the newer ones were built with cold-molded—rather than traditional plank-on-frame—construction, all but one have retained the original gaff rig. That means that there are running backstays to tend, because the long boom precludes a permanent backstay.

Dyon

52'6" x 13'0" • Designed by Luders & Smith • Built by Luders Marine Constr. Co. • Stamford, Connecticut • 1924

OWNED BY THE SAME FAMILY SINCE SHE WAS BUILT, *Dyon* still has her original name and gaff rig. As for mainte-nance, if all wooden boats could have been treated as well, there'd be many more survivors. She's always been stored in a shed, for example, where it's damp so her planking doesn't dry out. *Dyon* has never had, and still doesn't need, a rebuilding; she's a time capsule, and a monument to consistent good care.

Chips

50'3" x 10'3" P-class sloop • Designed by W. Starling Burgess • Built by W. Starling Burgess Corp. • Marblehead, MA • 1913

CHIPS WAS LITTLE MORE THAN A HULK kept afloat by steady pumping and in desperate need of restoration when she was discovered and saved by a new owner. He gave her just what she needed: *Chips* was reborn, complete with elegant accommodations, a new cabin, and a rig that, while probably not an exact duplicate of the original, is nonetheless perfectly appropriate, having been based on similar yachts of the era.

Elfitz

31'0" x 7'3" Winter Harbor 21 • Designed by Burgess & Packard • Built by Geo. F. Lawley & Son • Neponset, MA • 1923

SHE NEVER LEFT WINTER HARBOR, the place in Maine for which the class was designed and built—a distinction only two in this nine-boat class can claim. The other seven had dispersed during the 1960s and '70s. The knockabouts (a name given to cabin daysailers of this size and era) returned in the 1980s, thanks to members of the Winter Harbor Yacht Club. Now the entire fleet of nine is back home, racing hard and looking good.

Owl

25'0" x 8'0" Wianno Senior • Designed by H. Manley Crosby • Built by Crosby Yacht Bldg. • Osterville, MA • 1974

SENIOR BOATS HAVE ENJOYED STEADY USE since the first batch was launched in 1914. Many, like *Owl*, were subsequently built in wood (the very latest are in fiberglass), and older boats were refurbished. Some were lost to storms, fires, and old age, but the racing has never let up. You'll still find most of them in the waters off Cape Cod's southern shore, not far from where they were built in Osterville.

Circe

28'5" x 7'6" Triangle • Designed by John G. Alden • Built by Graves Yacht Yard • Marblehead, MA • 1926

BIG MAINSAILS WITH LONG BOOMS WERE POPULAR well into the 1920s, but toward that decade's end, sailors and designers began recognizing the potential of headsails. Soon after the big mainsail/small jib Triangle class sloops began racing, jibs began a conspicuous increase in relative size. But regardless of changing styles or technological advances, the Triangle remains one of the very best of the one-design cabin dayboats.

Pixie

24'6" x 6'9" Watch Hill 15 • Designed by N.G. Herreshoff • Built by Herreshoff Mfg. Co. • Bristol, Rhode Island • 1922

MARCONI RIGS WERE BECOMING THE STYLE when the Watch Hill 15s came out. So rigged, a boat like this, compared to her older, gaff-rigged sisters, would have one less halyard. Offsetting this would be the need for another pair of shrouds and longer spreaders to support the taller mast. There was little difference in cost or performance. It was keeping up with the prevailing fashion that justified the switch.

Quisset

15'10" x 5'10" Herreshoff 12½ • Designed by N.G. Herreshoff • Built by Herreshoff Mfg. Co. • Bristol, RI • 1928

THE GAFF-RIGGED AND MARCONI-RIGGED BOATS OF THIS DESIGN RACE TOGETHER, their average speeds are so alike. Between 1914 and 1945 when the Herreshoff Mfg. Co. closed its doors for good, 365 of these Herreshoff 12½-footers, fitted out with both kinds of rigs, were built—setting in motion a trend that shows no sign of a letup. They're still in production.

Shimmer

14'0" x 5'0" Biscayne Bay 14 • Designed by N.G. Herreshoff • Built by Eric Dow • Brooklin, Maine • 1988

SHE HANDLES LIKE A THOROUGHBRED, though she's called a sailing skiff. Her sails are big enough for speed in light air, and to help her carry that much area when it's windy there's a shallow, lead-ballast keel. There is elegant delicacy to all her many pieces—from the hollow, tapered mast to the wandlike tiller. The mainsail, although attached low on the mast, cocks up as it runs aft and gives the person at the tiller all-round visibility.

Curlew

26'0" x 7'7" • Designed by N.G. Herreshoff • Built by Customary Boats • Westport, Massachusetts • 1994

A SLIDING GUNTER MAINSAIL on this lovely *Alerion* replica allows a long leading edge, for sailing efficiency, without requiring the longer mast of a marconi sail. The single wire halyard runs from the gunter yard through a masthead sheave, down the mast to a single block through which passes the line used to hoist and lower the sail. There's a jig on one end of that hoisting line for fine-tuning after the sail has been raised.

S-Boats

27'6" x 7'2" • Designed by N.G. Herreshoff • Built by Herreshoff Mfg. Co. • Bristol, Rhode Island • 1919–1941

IN 1919, THE FIRST S-BOATS HERALDED THE MARCONI RIG'S ARRIVAL. Before then, nearly all sailing craft, boats and yachts alike, had been fitted with gaff sails. In the course of two decades, the Herreshoff yard turned out about 85 S-boats to a single, easily recognizable design. You can't mistake that gently curved mast, the cabin that comes to a point at its forward end, or the distinctive snubbed bow.

Neith

53'3" x 10'6" • Designed by N.G. Herreshoff • Built by Herreshoff Mfg. Co. • Bristol, Rhode Island • 1907

SHE CARRIES A PERMANENT BACKSTAY NOW, whereas the long boom of her original gaff mainsail wouldn't have cleared such a stay. Permanent backstays prevent the mast from bending forward and breaking when the wind is aft of abeam. *Neith* also has running backstays—two pair, in fact—for applying tension to keep the headsail luffs tight. She's sailing here without a forestaysail, so the lower runners aren't in use.

Dolphin

35'6" x 10'6" Newport 29 • Designed by N.G. Herreshoff • Built by Herreshoff Mfg. Co. • Bristol, Rhode Island • 1914

MORE HEEL DOESN'T ALWAYS MEAN MORE SPEED, as *Dolphin*'s skipper knows. He's tucked a reef into the mainsail so he can carry it full of wind without the leeward deck going underwater and dragging down the boat speed. Like *Neith*, *Dolphin*'s rig was changed from gaff to marconi and her headsail gained in height. And she, too, has both kinds of backstays—permanent and runners.

Eio

26'0" x 8'4" spidsgatter • Designed by Aage Utzon • Built by Lilles • Elsinore, Denmark • 1936

KNOWN FOR THEIR TALL RIGS, genuine *spidsgatters* come from 1930s Denmark, virtually all of them having been designed by Berg, Hanson, or Utzon. A few, such as these three shown sailing off Port Townsend, Washington, were shipped to the San Francisco and Seattle areas. These aren't one-designs, but their distinctive, high-crowned cabintops and wide, double-ended hulls make them easy to spot despite the variations.

Buttercup

26'0" x 9'0" • Designed by K. Aage Nielsen • Built by A. Walsted Baadevaerft • Thurø, Denmark • 1966

BUTTERCUP IS EVEN WIDER than a traditional *spidsgatter*, but she surely shares the same origins. In fact, her designer grew up in Denmark and studied under *spidsgatter* designer Georg Berg before moving to the United States. *Buttercup* comes from a later era, which accounts for her masthead rig, inboard rudder with wheel rather than tiller steering, and higher (for full standing headroom) cabin.

Free Spirit

33'4" x 9'8" Concordia 33 • Designed by Concordia Co. • Built by Palmer Scott/Ferguson • Fairhaven, MA • 1948

THE PERFECT BREEZE is one that heels a boat just enough for the lee rail to skim the water. Any more and it's time to think about reefing. Originally designed with a single jib set on a stay that ran from the tip of the bowsprit to about three-quarters of the way up the mast, the subsequent addition of the masthead yankee jib shown here gets her going—rail down, perfect breeze—in lighter winds.

Clover

29'7" x 8'0" Gulfstream 30 • Designed by Sparkman & Stephens, Inc. • Built by Robert E. Derecktor • Mamaroneck, NY • 1958

A MASTHEAD RIG is one in which the jibstay goes all the way to the top of the mast. Among its advantages are its simplicity and the ability to carry the biggest possible spinnaker downwind. Here, the headsail, not the mainsail, provides most of the drive—*Clover*'s mainsail serves as much to balance the helm as to drive the boat, so the feel of the tiller best determines the trim of the mainsail.

Rebellion

33'0" x 8'0" • Designed by Edmund Cutts • Built by Cutts & Case • Oxford, Maryland • 1966

SYNTHETIC SAILCLOTH MAKES TALL, NARROW SAILS POSSIBLE; a jib of this shape made of canvas would stretch too much. For easy handling, *Rebellion*'s self-tending jib can't be beat. Though tall, it sets perfectly, and the sheet need not be touched when changing tacks. Another fine feature is the all-round visibility from the cockpit. *Rebellion* is so much fun to sail that it's easy to understand why her builder decided to keep her.

Lorraine

25'0" x 7'2" Folkboat • Designed by Iversen & Sunden • Built by T.H. Lind • Middlefart, Denmark • 1959

THE NAUTICAL EQUIVALENT OF THE VOLKSWAGEN, countless Folkboats were built in Scandinavia, and many were shipped to the United States. *Lorraine* is one of the best-kept of all. With easy lines, a snug cabin with sleeping for two, a sensible rig, a traditional lapstrake hull, and harmonious proportions, it's no wonder that Folkboats were once nearly as popular as their automobile counterparts.

Inismara

41'6" x 9'9" • Designed by James McGruer • Built by McGruer & Co., Ltd. • Clynder, Dunbarton, Scotland • 1963

YOU CAN SEE UNDER A JIB LIKE THIS if you're at the helm, and if you're taking the boat's picture, you can see its foredeck. Although the Scottish landscape here is very lovely, we wanted to show as much of this handsome McGruer sloop as possible and not have it hidden behind a low-cut genoa. *Inismara*'s owners graciously complied with our request, and her speed barely faltered after the headsail change.

Dram

33'2" x 6'9" International One-Design • Designed and built by Bjarne Aas • Fredrikstad, Norway • 1937

A SPINNAKER HELPS PULL A BOAT DOWNWIND better than a jib because it's bigger. The wind velocity that a boat feels drops off dramatically when the boat goes from being close-hauled to sailing downwind, so racers add area by setting a spinnaker. Anything goes when it comes to spinnaker color and pattern, so you're likely to see a wide variation even in a fleet of one-designs like the Internationals.

Gleam

67'11" x 12'0" 12 meter • Designed by Clinton H. Crane • Built by Henry B. Nevins, Inc. • City Island, New York • 1937

NEWPORT, RHODE ISLAND, BOASTS A FLEET OF 12-METER SLOOPS that would do any harbor proud. But, unlike the other Twelves, many of which were involved with the *America*'s Cup competition, *Gleam* was built with cruising accommodations right from the beginning. Her designer was her first owner, and although he enjoyed racing, he also liked to cruise—so she's among the more practical boats of the class.

Astra

115'0" x 20'2" J-class sloop • Designed by C.E. Nicholson • Built by Camper & Nicholson, Ltd. • Gosport, England • 1928

ALWAYS IMPRESSIVE BECAUSE OF THEIR SIZE, modern sailing yachts this big are not often as beautiful as this one. Aesthetics was an unspoken priority back when *Astra* was built, whereas today that's changed. Now it tends to be accommodations and performance that get the most attention. But the good news is that classic yachts like *Astra* still attract owners with the interest and means to keep them sailing.

Rosie Parks

46'2" x 16'7" skipjack • Modeled & built by Bronza Parks • Wingate, Maryland • 1955

THIS SKIPJACK RETIRED EARLY and now belongs to the Chesapeake Bay Maritime Museum of St. Michaels, Maryland. Used mostly as a floating dockside exhibit, *Rosie* still occasionally sails. Speed to windward isn't a priority for skipjacks, so their sails are given neither roach nor battens. The cloths run parallel with the leech for strength and there are reefs aplenty—*Rosie* has two more besides the one that's tied in.

Maggie Lee

51'0" x 16'0" skipjack • Built in Pocomoke, Virginia • 1903

SKIPJACKS ARE DELIBERATELY SLOWED DOWN IN HIGH WINDS BY REEFING because the dredge can't be towed too fast over an oyster bed and still pick up a good catch. When dredging, it's always a beam reach, but for getting to and from the oyster beds the motorized pushboat is lowered and put to use. Except for a couple of days each week when it's legal to use the pushboats over the beds, the dredging must be done under sail.

Banjo

28'0" x 10'0" • Modeled and built by Buckley Smith • Brooklin, Maine • 1981

DECKED-OVER SCOW SLOOPS HAVE A TRANSOM AT EACH END so they can carry a large deck load. The boom, carried high for headroom and visibility, can be raised even more by reefing the sail, if necessary, in order to clear unusually high loads. *Banjo*'s cargoes are apt to be anything from sawn lumber to a group of music-makers, to a tractor, or even a horse. A tent, pitched on deck, provides shelter for sleeping aboard this versatile craft.

Unity B

34'0" x 12'0" • Modeled and built by Alfred Bain • Lisbon Creek, Mangrove Cay, Bahamas • 1950

THE MAINSAIL HEADBOARD ACTS ALMOST LIKE A GAFF, even though hoisted on a single halyard. Bahamian reefing, as you can see, is basic and amounts to bundling up and tying the lower corners of both mainsail and jib so there's less sail to hoist. It's not ideal, especially for sailing to windward, but it's quick and effective in boats that sail on a reach most of the time.

Nuovo Mondo

18'6" x 7'0" felucca replica • Built by Larry Hitchcock • San Francisco, California • 1987

IMMIGRANT ITALIAN FISHERMEN CHOSE FELUCCAS when they landed in San Francisco and resumed fishing. Immigrant Italian boatbuilders complied and, before long, hundreds of these Mediterranean-style double-enders were in use. Now only traces of the felucca era remain. *Nuovo Mondo* is a replica of this nearly lost, lateen-rigged craft, built for hands-on research.

Yachts of Friesland

Typically 20'0" x 8'6" (Friese jachten) and 30'0" x 13'0" (boeiers) • Built in Friesland, Netherlands • From ca. 1870

DUTCH YACHTS ARE UNLIKE ANY OTHERS, and one of the reasons is that the sailing conditions there are unusual. The waters are always shallow and rarely rough, so the hulls can be shoal-bodied, bluff-ended, and wide. Leeboards work well, taking the place of keels or centerboards. Sail plans are high to catch the wind above the canal embankments. The beauty of these traditional sailing craft is as appealing as their uniqueness.

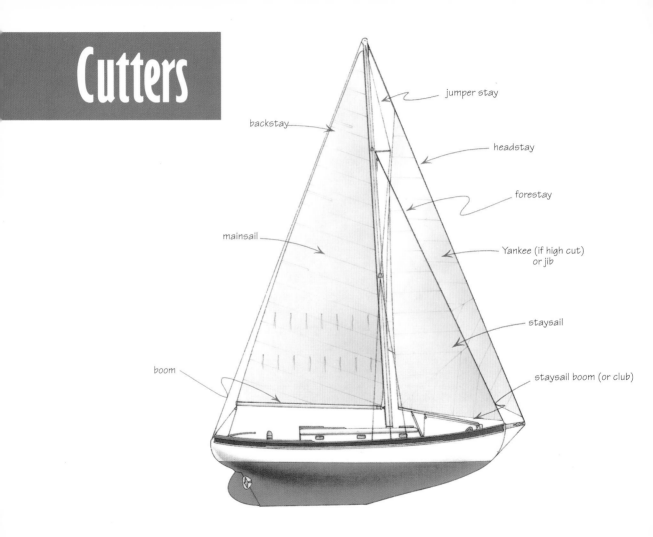

Cutters

jumper stay

backstay

headstay

forestay

mainsail

Yankee (if high cut)
or jib

staysail

boom

staysail boom (or club)

A century ago the term cutter designated the type of hull as much as the rig, but for many years now, the term has been used for *a single-masted boat having more than one headsail whose mast is stepped nearer amidships than a sloop's.* "Nearer amidships" is a vague description and there are some rigs that could be described either way. The designer's designation counts, and so does the owner's, and, when in doubt, it's best to acquiesce to those authorities.

Because the sail area is shared among three (and sometimes four) sails, the size of the mainsail (the largest) is less than in a sloop of the same total area, and this makes it easier to handle. Offsetting this is the added gear that goes with the extra headsail. If the staysail (the smaller and aftermost of the two headsails) uses a boom, however, there is a single sheet which doesn't need tending when tacking.

When reefed, cutters stay balanced better than sloops, because dropping the jib (the larger, forwardmost headsail) compensates for the reef in the mainsail.

More often than not, cutters have bowsprits and short forward overhangs. (*Baccarat*, page 63, is the only exception herein). There's a propensity toward a gaff mainsail in wooden cutters, as well. Above the gaff, some cutters set a topsail for added push in light winds. You're more likely to see a separate (fidded) topmast on a cutter (as with *Bryony* and *Anne Marie II*, pages 70 and 71) than on a sloop.

Able

24'0" x 8'11" • Designed by Lyle Hess • Built by Bertram Levy • Port Townsend, Washington • 1984

SOME SAILORS DON'T LIKE ENGINES and would rather take their chances without one. There's really no risk if you know how to sail; it's the inconvenience of not being able to hold to a schedule that's the drawback. A long sculling oar, *Able*'s only auxiliary power, pushes her slowly when there's no wind. But on a morning this beautiful, schedules are kind of hard to think about.

Vito Dumas

31'0" x 10'4" • Designed by Manuel Campos • Built by Carlos Parodi • Buenos Aires, Argentina • 1933

LARGER THAN *ABLE*, AND FITTED WITH AN INBOARD ENGINE, this cutter shares the same Port Townsend waters. She's still small enough for singlehanding, and today she and her owner are off on a cruise out through the Strait of Juan de Fuca—the early morning start timed to make the tide.

Jarges Pride

33'0" x 9'6" • Designed by S. S. Crocker • Built by Donald Bugden • Beverly, Massachusetts • 1970

EVENING SAILS ARE SOMETIMES THE NICEST, or at least the most relaxing, because then the wind is dropping, not rising. Earlier, *Jarges Pride* was rail down; now, in a more moderate breeze, sailing is ideal, and by darkness, she'll waft home on what's left of the afternoon's westerly. It's this kind of after-work sailing that makes all the maintenance worthwhile.

Baccarat

46'4" x 11'0" • Designed and built by Russell J. Pouliot • Detroit, Michigan • 1933

***BACCARAT* HAS SAILED MANY MILES WITH ONLY HER OWNER ABOARD**—and all of them without benefit of engine or self-steering. She's not your typical singlehander, and to manage a boat this big alone, one has to be a first-class seaman who not only knows the boat thoroughly, but is expert at navigation and weather prediction. The sails are big and the anchor heavy, so *Baccarat* demands physical strength as well.

Northern Crown

35'6" x 11'5" • Designed by K. Aage Nielsen • Built by A. Walsted Baadevaerft • Thurø, Denmark • 1956

NORTHERN CROWN'S CREW HAS DECIDED TO LOWER AND FURL HER SAILS—except for the flasher, a downwind, light-air sail that's gently pulling this double-ender to her nearby anchorage. The wind is so light and the sea so calm that they'll drop the flasher and let the anchor go on-the-fly, without bothering to round up, allowing the boat's momentum to dig it in.

Sweet Olive

43'0" x 12'0" • Designed by Joel White • Built by Brooklin Boat Yard • Brooklin, Maine • 1991

FLASHERS ARE LIKE SPINNAKERS WITHOUT POLES—asymmetrical, with a luff that's longer than the leech. All that's required to set them is to belay the tack line to the stem or bowsprit, reeve the sheet through a fairlead near the cockpit, snap on the halyard, hoist away, and trim the sheet until the sail fills. It's a quick way to add off-the-wind sail area without the complications of a true spinnaker and its pole.

Skye

31'8" x 10'8" • Designed by Lyle Hess • Built by William & Elaine Eppick • Aloha, Oregon • 1988

***SKYE* IS *ABLE*'S BIG SISTER** and, with the same seakindly hull shape, is equally capable of making long ocean passages. Reefing the mainsail at sea, or furling it altogether, is safer and easier because of the gallows frame, which holds the outboard end of the boom secure. Opinions vary on staysail booms, but *Skye*'s staysail sets better without one.

Mimi Rose

32'0" x 10'0" • Designed by Robert H. Baker & Joel White • Built by Gordon Swift & William Page • Exeter, NH • 1991

REEFING A CUTTER'S MAINSAIL IS A GOOD FIRST STEP IN SHORTENING SAIL when the wind breezes up. It will not only reduce the heeling and the overall stress on the rig, but will lessen the weather helm as well. Alternatively, if you lowered and furled one of the headsails, you'd relieve the boat, but you would throw her out of balance and she'd carry an excessive weather helm.

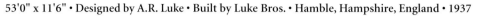

Shiris

53'0" x 11'6" • Designed by A.R. Luke • Built by Luke Bros. • Hamble, Hampshire, England • 1937

ROLLER REEFING IS ANOTHER WAY OF REDUCING A MAINSAIL'S SIZE. It's like rolling up a window shade: You simultaneously rotate the boom (with a cranking device at the gooseneck) and slack the halyard. *Shiris*'s reefed mainsail has retained its shape, but often that doesn't happen and the sail loses its drive. That's one reason so-called jiffy reefing is more common now.

Arawak

44'8" x 12'3" • Designed by W. Starling Burgess • Built by Eastern Shipbuilding Corp. • Shelburne, N.S., Canada • 1931

KNOWN FOR MOST OF HER LIFE AS *CHRISTMAS,* this double-ender's potential for speed increased dramatically when she was given a larger sail plan, a lightweight carbon fiber mast with rod rigging, and a heavier ballast keel. While such conversions make old wooden boats speedier in light and moderate conditions, it's important not to drive them beyond reason when the going gets rough.

Bryony

34'0" x 10'0" • Designed by Jim Franken • Built by N.W. School of Wooden Boatbuilding • Port Townsend, WA • 1983

JACKYARD TOPSAILS USED TO BE THE ACCEPTED WAY to give a cutter more sail area. Nowadays, if a gaff topsail is used at all, it's usually without a sprit or jackyard, and can't extend beyond the top of the mast or the end of the gaff. Too bad, not only because it's a less spectacular sight than *Bryony*, but without that extra area the topsail isn't as effective.

Anne Marie II

57'0" x 12'6" • Designed by Enos Harris • Built by Harris Bros. • Rowhedge, Essex, England • 1911

AN ELEGANT YACHT OF THE EDWARDIAN ERA MAKES A COMFORTABLE FLOATING HOME, and that's just where this cutter's owners have decided to live. Luckily for the boat and for those of us who see her, these folks fully appreciate the treasure they have acquired and are slowly and appropriately restoring her. When finished, she'll once again carry the original, and much larger, sail plan.

Masuyo

32'6" x 9'8" • Designed and built by David Howarth • Shetland Islands, Scotland • 1951

HEAVY, SEAGOING BOATS LIKE THIS NEARLY FLY WITH A STRONG WIND BEHIND THEM, and it's smart to take advantage of such weather. Experienced cruisers don't beat to windward unless they have to; neither their boats nor their rigs are made for it. But a long and slippery state-of-the-art racer, designed for on-the-wind performance, wouldn't have *Masuyo*'s easy motion. Tradeoffs and compromises abound when it comes to boats.

Morning Star

39'6" x 11'6" Galway hooker • Modeled and built by Patrick Brannelly • Kinvara, Galway, Ireland • 1884

WITH HULL SHAPES THAT ARE NOW TWO CENTURIES OUT OF DATE, hookers carried both passengers and freight between villages of southwestern Ireland before there were trucks and automobiles. Their mainsails are loose-footed (attached to the boom only at the forward and aft corners) and laced to the mast, instead of having hoops. They're very basic workboats, with simple outboard rudders and tillers for steering.

Lizzie Annie

34'0" x 11'0" • Essex smack • Built in Brightlingsea, Essex, England • 1906

HER BOWSPRIT CAN BE HOUSED—pulled inboard—so as to be out of the way when the vessel is laying to a dock. Doing so is a matter of knocking out the transverse pin that bears against the bitts; the bowsprit can then slide aft until most of it lies on deck inboard of the stem. Reefing bowsprits, as useful as they are, are not seen on many yachts.

Hirta

46'0" x 13'8" • Bristol Channel pilot cutter • Designed and built by J. Slade & Sons • Fowey, Cornwall, England • 1911

BOATS DON'T GET MUCH SEAWORTHIER THAN *HIRTA* and her many, and now mostly vanished, sisters that used to patrol England's busy and stormy Bristol Channel. These cutters were at sea most of the time, winter or summer, fair weather or foul. Pilots lived aboard until they picked up an inbound vessel or came back aboard after they got dropped off from an outbound one.

Yawls

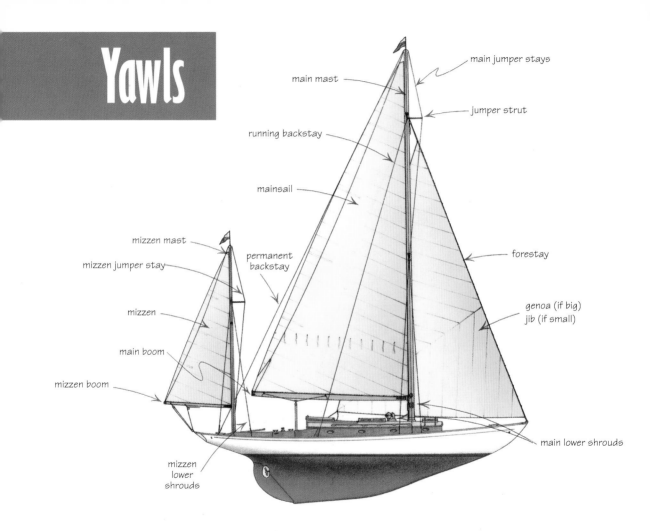

main mast

main jumper stays

jumper strut

running backstay

mainsail

mizzen mast

permanent backstay

mizzen jumper stay

forestay

mizzen

genoa (if big)
jib (if small)

main boom

mizzen boom

main lower shrouds

mizzen lower shrouds

Yawls have two masts, and the mainmast (the forward one) is by far the tallest. Technically, to be a yawl, the mizzenmast must be stepped aft of the rudderstock. You can think of a yawl as a sloop with an extra little sail aft; that is, most of the drive comes from the mainsail and headsail.

A yawl's mizzen, even though it doesn't have much drive, is still a worthwhile sail and its role shouldn't be underrated. While sailing, the mizzen sheet can be adjusted to ease the steering. (Slacked if there's too much weather helm; pulled in if there's not enough.) Dropping and furling a yawl's mizzen altogether is often equivalent to a single reef in the mainsail—and a whole lot quicker and easier to execute.

Sheeted tight, with the mainsail and jib sheets cast off, a mizzen will weathercock the boat and keep her head-to-wind. That's a great comfort when picking up a mooring or paying out scope after anchoring. There's no sailing around, first on one tack, then the other, as is often the case with a sloop.

As with certain sloops and cutters, it's sometimes hard to differentiate between a yawl and a ketch. But, as with some single-mast rigs, it's best to leave the rig designation of those gray-area boats to the designer or the owner.

Quill II

38'0" x 9'10" • Designed by B.B. Crowninshield • Built by Hodgdon Bros. • East Boothbay, Maine • 1905

A RARE SIGHT NOWADAYS is a yawl carrying gaff sails on both her masts. Although a natural companion to her rig, the round-fronted trunk cabin is nearly as uncommon. *Quill II* has the distinction of being the oldest extant yacht built by the famed Hodgdon yard of East Boothbay, Maine.

Annie

24'0" x 8'6" • Designed by Fenwick C. Williams • Built by Arundel Shipyard • Kennebunkport, Maine • 1980

CALLED A TABLOID CRUISER because of her compact size and condensed accommodations, this double-ender carries her mizzenmast well aft so it's clear of the cockpit. This boat's mizzen is so small that the mast can stand alone without the customary shrouds for support, and, even though it steps ahead of the rudder, it is aft of the helm—making her a yawl.

Dorade

52'0"x 10'3" • Designed by Sparkman & Stephens, Inc. • Built by Minneford Yacht Yard • City Island, New York • 1930

***DORADE* MADE YACHTING HISTORY** as the first of the successful ocean racers to be rigged as a marconi yawl. Not only did she influence the style of yachts to follow, but she made famous the names of Olin and Rod Stephens, the brothers who conceived her and sailed her, as the family yacht, to her first string of victories.

Stormy Weather

53'11" x 12'6" • Designed by Sparkman & Stephens, Inc. • Built by Henry B. Nevins, Inc. • City Island, New York • 1934

INSPIRED BY *DORADE*'S SUCCESS, the Stephens brothers refined the hull shape when designing *Stormy Weather*. Both yachts clearly demonstrated that yawls could not only win races consistently but also go to sea as safely and comfortably as the schooners that were the previous decade's favored rig.

Cirrus

44'0" x 10'9" Fishers Island 31 • Designed & built by Herreshoff Mfg. Co. • Bristol, Rhode Island • 1930

CONVERTED FROM SLOOP TO YAWL for easier handling, *Cirrus* has been homeported in Brooklin, Maine, for nearly 70 years. She's undeniably fast in any company, despite still having spliced-eye standing rigging holding up her original hollow spruce mast. Her main boom is the one that she's always had as well, although it's been shortened to allow for the mizzen and permanent backstay.

Athene

63'4" x 13'10" • Designed by Sparkman & Stephens, Inc. • Built by Henry B. Nevins, Inc. • City Island, New York • 1937

RECOGNIZABLE BY HER DISTINCTIVE DECKHOUSE, this San Francisco-based yawl was launched as *Elizabeth McCaw* for East Coast ocean racing. *Athene* evolved from *Dorade* and *Stormy Weather* and shares their deep-hull advantage of full standing headroom under an essentially flush deck.

Desperate Lark

49'10" x 10'6" Bar Harbor 31 • Designed by N.G. Herreshoff • Built by Herreshoff Mfg. Co. • Bristol, Rhode Island • 1903

SPREADING A SPINNAKER KEEPS THIS OLD GIRL MOVING when the wind comes abaft the beam. This kind of special downwind sail would be less necessary if *Desperate Lark* still carried her original gaff sloop rig with its huge mainsail and double headsails. That old rig called for a professional crew with plenty of muscle. Now, as a snugly rigged marconi yawl, she's virtually a singlehander—as long as the spinnaker is left in the bag!

Madrigal

46'0" x 11'11" • Designed by Sparkman & Stephens, Inc. • Built by Paul E. Luke • East Boothbay, Maine • 1958

A MIZZEN STAYSAIL IS ANOTHER DOWNWIND SAIL often used on yawls which, combined with a spinnaker, nearly doubles the sail area. Both sails call for special handling when jibing. The spinnaker pole must shift sides, and the staysail has to be lowered and rigged from the new leeward side, then rehoisted.

Sula

40'0" x 11'3" • Designed by Sparkman & Stephens, Inc. • Built by Henry B. Nevins, Inc. • City Island, New York • 1959

MASTHEAD YAWLS WITH CENTERBOARDS BECAME THE STYLE of the 1950s and '60s. Racing is by handicap in boats this size and the handicapping formula then in vogue favored a wide boat with a yawl rig, bestowing her a lower rating. The overlapping portion of headsails wasn't part of the calculation, nor were spinnakers or mizzen staysails, so, at the time, it paid racing dividends to have a rig as well as a wide hull like *Sula*'s.

Rogue

37'0" x 10'6" • Designed by N.G. Herreshoff • Built by Seth Persson • Saybrook, Connecticut • 1953

IN THE DISTANCE WE SPOTTED A SAIL as well as an ominous black cloud. The sail proved to belong to *Rogue*—one of Herreshoff's great Newport 29s with a yawl rig—much more than we'd hoped for. The sky proved less than feared and the sun soon poked through to highlight *Rogue*'s sails as she arrived at Nassau.

Infanta

47'0" x 11'8" • Designed by Philip L. Rhodes • Built by Kretzer Boat Works, Inc. • City Island, New York • 1947

TWO HEADSAILS INSTEAD OF ONE make for easier handling on larger yachts, especially if a boom is fitted to the staysail so there's no sheet to tend for that sail when tacking. When an increasing wind calls for shortening sail, the forwardmost headsail—called a yankee—can be lowered and furled or replaced with one that's smaller.

Stephen Nason

30'0" x 9'8" Malabar Jr. • Designed by John G. Alden • Built by The Landing School • Kennebunkport, Maine • 1990

TACKING IS EASY because the jib, fitted with a boom, is self-tending, as are the mainsail and mizzen. That is to say that all three sails on this lovely Malabar Jr. flop over from one side to the other automatically when the boat passes through the eye of the wind and sets off on the other tack. All you have to do is steer.

Kay

51'4" x 13'6" • Designed by Sparkman & Stephens, Inc. • Built by A. Walsted Baadevaerft • Thurø, Denmark • 1977

DESIGNED FOR COMFORT AND SAFETY AT SEA, *Kay* replaces a nearly identical yacht that her owner sold to an admirer before completion. It was a gracious move, but one that enabled some subtle improvements to this, his second boat. *Kay*'s mainsail and mizzen can be reefed by rotating their booms so the sails roll up like window shades. For downwind sailing, the whisker pole can be swung down to hold out the jib clew.

Violet

45'8" x 13'3" converted Scottish zulu • Built by the James Noble yard • Fraserburgh, Scotland • 1911

STRICTLY SPEAKING, *VIOLET* COULD BE CLASSIFIED A KETCH because her mizzen steps forward of the rudder. But in terms of the relative size of her sails, she's more like a yawl—thus her placement in this chapter. Originally, however, *Violet* carried a dipping lugsail on the mainmast and a slightly smaller standing lugsail on the main. Without doubt, in those days she was a ketch.

Tioga

50'0" x 12'7" • Designed by K. Aage Nielsen • Built by Cantieri Baglietto • Varazze, Italy • 1954

ROLLING UP A HEADSAIL IS QUICK compared to lowering and furling it or stuffing it into a sailbag. No one has to leave the cockpit. You simply take a few turns around a convenient winch with the rolling-up pennant and crank in on it while someone casts off and slacks away on the sheets. With low-friction swivels top and bottom, the headsail becomes a neat roll in a matter of seconds.

Red Head

28'0" x 6'4" Rozinante canoe yawl • Designed by L. Francis Herreshoff • Built by Benjamin River Marine • Brooklin, Maine • 1994

MINOR CHANGES MADE HER A YAWL. The yawl devotee justifiably boasts that the mizzen doesn't clutter up the cockpit. Although *Red Head* was designed as a ketch, an 18-inch relocation of the mizzen toward the stern and a slight lengthening of the afterdeck so it could serve as a mast step turned her into a yawl. As you can see, she'll still steer herself occasionally without a hand on the tiller.

Pacifica

48'9" x 11'0" • Designed by Sparkman & Stephens, Inc. • Built by Henry B. Nevins, Inc. • City Island, New York • 1947

LIKE *ATHENE,* *PACIFICA* SAILED ALONG THE EAST COAST before relocating to California waters and undergoing an appropriate name change. Launched as *Eroica*, this lovely yawl has benefited from having a succession of good owners who have kept her in topnotch condition. They understand that, no matter where a yacht is located, she has to have consistent care based on an understanding of both the boat and the environment.

Odyssey

58'0" x 13'9" • Designed by I. Judson Kelly • Built by Stephens Bros. • Stockton, California • 1938

FROM CALIFORNIA YOU CAN SAIL WEST FOR WEEKS before sighting land, but first you have to open up an empty horizon by clearing Catalina and a couple of other off-lying islands. And whether to Catalina or on to Tahiti, *Odyssey* is up to the voyage. The Stephens yard of Stockton, known primarily for high-grade power cruisers, created a fine sailing yacht in *Odyssey*.

Nirvana

65'0" x 14'3" • Designed by John G. Alden • Built by Henry R. Hinckley & Co. • Southwest Harbor, Maine • 1950

ORIGINALLY OWNED AND SAILED WITHIN SIGHT OF THE BUILDER'S YARD in Southwest Harbor, Maine, *Nirvana* has come to call Newport, Rhode Island, her home port in recent years. But even many miles from her building site, those distinctive covestripe endings reveal her lineage—and that of *Windigo* as well.

Windigo

73'3" x 15'5" • Designed by Sparkman & Stephens, Inc. • Built by Henry R. Hinckley & Co. • Southwest Harbor, ME • 1956

THE BIGGEST WOODEN SAILING YACHT HINCKLEY HAD EVER BUILT, *Windigo* was commissioned by the same man who had *Nirvana* built. Several owners and 30 years later, *Windigo* still looks like new sailing in the Antigua Classic Yacht Regatta, where she competes with such racing legends as *Ticonderoga* and *Stormy Weather*.

Hallowe'en

71'3" x 14'6" • Designed by W. & R.B. Fife • Built by William Fife & Son • Fairlie, Scotland • 1926

WILLIAM FIFE HAD A GOOD EYE FOR HULL SHAPE and the yachts built at the Fife yard in Scotland combine delicate beauty with a robustness that few other designers have matched. This big yawl, long known in the States as *Cotton Blossom IV*, is a fine example. No matter what rig she's fitted with—and she's had several versions of yawl—she exudes elegance in a hearty sort of way.

Escapade

72'6" x 17'1" • Designed by Philip L. Rhodes • Built by Luders Marine Constr. Co. • Stamford, Connecticut • 1938

A YAWL OFFERS VARIOUS WAYS OF SHORTENING SAIL when the wind pipes up, and all three of *Escapade*'s working sails (staysail, mainsail, and mizzen) can be reefed, adding even more options. For instance, if snugged down to only a triple-reefed mainsail and reefed staysail, she'd be under storm sails—in effect, the same as a storm trysail and spitfire jib—and would be ready for a really big wind.

Starlight

39'10" x 10'0" • Designed by Concordia Co., Inc. • Built by Abeking & Rasmussen • Lemwerder, Germany • 1954

CHANCES ARE IT'S A CONCORDIA if you see a yawl with a sweet sheer and a notably small mizzen. More than 100 were built and all are still sailing. They are homeported far and wide, and there are few places in the country they haven't raced or cruised. If you're at all in doubt about the identity, look for the star at the bow and the crescent moon at the stern.

Aida

33'6" x 9'2" • Designed by N.G. Herreshoff • Built by Herreshoff Mfg. Co. • Bristol, Rhode Island • 1926

A FLAT-SHEETED MIZZEN WEATHERCOCKS THE BOAT, holding her head-to-wind for all kinds of operations, whether it's quietly lying to an anchor or backing downwind with certainty after you've just dropped one. Add a jib and you've got a heavy-weather sail combination, or, if the mizzen is dropped with the other two sails up, you have, almost instantly, the equivalent of a single reef. You guessed it: The yawl is my favorite rig!

Ketches

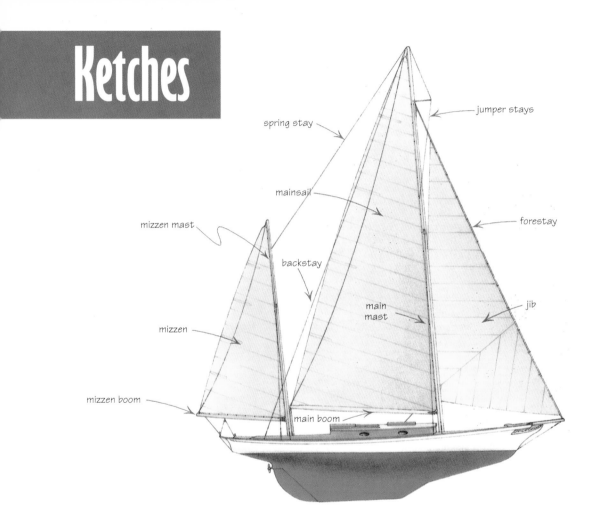

spring stay

jumper stays

mainsail

forestay

mizzen mast

backstay

mizzen

main mast

jib

mizzen boom

main boom

A ketch is much like a yawl, only with a larger mizzen whose mast steps forward of the rudderstock. For most cruising boats, this places the mast in the middle of the cockpit and is, to some, one of the primary disadvantages of a ketch rig. The other is, of course, the ineffectiveness of the mizzen sail due to its being in the wind shadow of the mainsail when closehauled. A yawl's mizzen suffers similarly, but, because its mainsail and jib are proportionally larger than those of a ketch, a yawl's luffing mizzen makes less difference in on-the-wind speed.

On the other side of the coin, a ketch maintains better balance when the mainsail is reefed or furled because the mizzen is more nearly equal to the jib in area. And because of its proportionally shorter mainmast and main boom, the jib and mainsail are smaller than in a yawl and easier to hoist and furl. Deep-water cruisers not preoccupied with speed favor ketches over yawls and sloops. (Recently, however, a new generation of ketches with tall, narrow mainsails and mizzens, separated from each other enough to keep the mizzen in clear air, have become popular in the big-boat race circuit.)

Both gaff and marconi ketches are popular in wood, and occasionally you see a ketch with a combination of the two. Ketches without headsails are, logically, cat ketches and these variant rigs can also have gaff or marconi sails and, occasionally, other sail types such as the gunter sails that the sailing canoe *Twilite* (page 122) carries.

Ticonderoga

72'0" x 16'0" • Designed by L. Francis Herreshoff • Built by Quincy Adams Yacht Yard • Quincy, Massachusetts • 1936

AMONG THE WORLD'S MOST BEAUTIFUL YACHTS, *Ticonderoga* adds class to any race, any anchorage, or anywhere else she appears. She's easily recognized by her raking masts, her clipper bow, elliptical transom, and raised quarter rail. The proportions, down to the smallest detail, are perfect—she is her designer's masterpiece.

Rosa II

40'11" x 10'4" • Designed by M. Rosenblatt & Son, Inc. • Built by Paul E. Luke • East Boothbay, Maine • 1960

CAREFULLY DESIGNED, EXQUISITELY BUILT, AND IMPECCABLY MAINTAINED, *Rosa II* was a father and son project. They created, on paper, the yacht of their dreams, selected the best builder they knew, and, in return, got one of the most uniquely beautiful ketches that ever sailed.

Sumurun

94'0" x 16'6" • Designed by William Fife III • Built by William Fife & Son • Fairlie, Scotland • 1914

A MIZZEN STAYSAIL ADDS A LOT OF PULL for off-the-wind sailing, especially in a ketch, and especially in a ketch as big as this. It's a serious sail, no doubt about it, and adds considerably to the speed. You'll rarely see a bigger ketch than this, or a lovelier one. The beauty of Fife's creations helps explain why so many have survived.

Belle Aventure

85'0" x 17'6" • Designed by W. & R.B. Fife • Built by William Fife & Son • Fairlie, Scotland • 1928

FORESTAYSAIL, JIB, AND JIB TOPSAIL ARE THE NAMES OF THESE HEADSAILS, working forward from the mainmast. Each has to be carefully trimmed so as not to backwind the sail astern, and, of course, each headsail has to be cast off and resheeted during a tack. But this charterboat's crew has all the moves well practiced, so any operation looks effortless.

Chautauqua

37'11" x 11'0" • Designed by S.S. Crocker • Built by Willis J. Reid • Winthrop, Massachusetts • 1928

IN A KETCH, YOU USUALLY HAVE TO SHARE THE COCKPIT WITH THE MIZZENMAST, but this is of little consequence to those who love the rig for its other merits. Because she's racing, *Chautauqua* has her genoa set and her working jib furled. But the breeze is getting stronger and, were the finish line not in sight, she'd be changing headsails about now.

Lands End

38'10" x 10'11" • Designed by S.S. Crocker • Built by Britt Bros. • West Lynn, Massachusetts • 1935

SHE'S SHED HER CONVENTIONAL MAINSAIL FOR ONE THAT ROLLS UP AGAINST THE MAST. It's like a roller-furling jib, but vertical, and with a boom along the foot of the sail. It's convenient to dowse the sail by slacking away the outhaul and cranking in on the furling line. But, because there can be no battens, there can be no roach—so some sail area is sacrificed.

Quiet Tune

29'6" x 7'10" • Designed by L. Francis Herreshoff • Built by Hodgdon Bros. • East Boothbay, Maine • 1945

HER COCKPIT IS SHALLOW AND WITHOUT SEATS, but it's surprisingly comfortable when you sprawl out on the cushions and lean against the coaming. From the tiller you can reach the main and mizzen sheets, and, if you're alone and have to tend the jibsheets, you don't have far to move. The visibility is great all around because you look out under the booms and over the low cabin.

Araminta

33'0" x 8'6" • Designed by L. Francis Herreshoff • Built by Norman Hodgdon • Boothbay Harbor, Maine • 1954

CREATED AS *QUIET TUNE*'S REPLACEMENT, the larger and more ornate *Araminta* had the same basic layout—from her shallow cockpit to her Spartan interior—but was subsequently transformed from daysailer to cruiser. Because *Araminta* sails as well as she looks, the design continues to be a favorite among those who like a boat that is both traditional and fast.

Mermaid

45'8" x 11'6" • Designed by Sparkman & Stephens, Inc. • Built by Paul E. Luke • East Boothbay, Maine • 1957

***MERMAID*'S RATING TAKES INTO ACCOUNT HER SPINNAKER** and the extra speed it provides. In handicap racing, the lower the rating relative to her competition, the more time a boat is allowed to sail around the racecourse. *Mermaid*'s spinnaker and mizzen staysail would have to cut about five minutes off the elapsed time over a 15-mile course to compensate for her higher rating.

Moonshine

58'6" x 14'4" • Designed and built by A.M. Dickie & Sons • Tarbert, Scotland • 1927

ONE SAIL'S TRIM MAY AFFECT ANOTHER, as *Moonshine*'s jib topsail shown here is backwinding the top of her mainsail. But, because size for size a headsail has more drive than a sail attached to a mast, *Moonshine*'s skipper may be giving priority to the jib topsail. This situation is about to change at the windward mark anyway, when the three headsails will be replaced by the reaching jib that's laid out on deck, ready for hoisting.

Patience B

36'0" x 10'6" • Designed by William H. Hand, Jr. • Built by Harry Bryan • Letete, N.B., Canada • 1988

FOR CRUISING THE SOUTH PACIFIC, the builder's family of four found *Patience B* to be just about the perfect boat. It's a design that dates from 1912, drawn by a man who clearly understood how to create a seaworthy hull and a rig to match. More recently, this little vessel has been used closer to home for teaching seamanship.

Alisande

36'0" x 10'2" • Designed by Wm. Hand & Joel White • Built by Brooklin Boat Yard • Brooklin, Maine • 1981

BUILT TO THE SAME BASIC DESIGN AS *PATIENCE B, Alisande* has proven to be a fine coastal cruiser. She'll drive to windward, but she—or any gaff ketch, for that matter—sails a lot faster on a reach when the sheets can be slacked a bit. It's blowing hard enough to reef here, but, because her mooring is only a short distance away, she'll get there by spilling wind from both mainsail and mizzen while the jib does most of the work.

Ayuthia

46'0" x 11'6" • Designed by Maurice Griffiths • Built by Alfred Harris • Bangkok, Thailand • 1936

MOVING FAST IN PERFECT COMFORT under only her forestaysail and full mainsail, *Ayuthia* demonstrates one of the many sail combinations possible with a ketch. The trick is knowing your boat and how she'll respond to the various options. The object is to keep her from being overpowered (too much sail set) while retaining a balanced helm.

Horizon

39'0" x 11'6" • Designed by John G. Alden • Built by George Luzier • Sarasota, Florida • 1968

SETTING ONLY THE JIB AND MIZZEN is another way of shortening sail in a ketch. Because she is only out for the afternoon and the breeze is strong, *Horizon*'s owners, quite sure they'll not be raising the mainsail, have left the sail cover in place. In fine-tuning the boat's balance to get a near-neutral helm, the jib has been deliberately overtrimmed.

Edna E. Lockwood

54'8" x 17'2" bugeye • Modeled and built by John B. Harrison • Tilghman Island, Maryland • 1889

A BUGEYE IS A SPECIAL KIND OF KETCH: The hull is double-ended at the waterline, but at deck level has a "patent," square stern with davits for hoisting the pushboat. Bugeyes predated skipjacks (pages 52 and 53) as Chesapeake Bay's oyster dredgers. Instead of plank-on-frame hulls, they're built of several logs fastened together and shaped to form the bottom, and with planks above to form the topsides.

Ring-Andersen

93'0" x 21'0" Baltic trader • Designed and built by Ring-Andersen Shipyard • Svendborg, Denmark • 1948

ORIGINALLY A COMMERCIAL FREIGHT CARRIER, *Ring-Andersen*'s role has changed to luxury charter yacht. Her rig, deck, and interior were altered during the conversion, and her sailing grounds are now Caribbean and Newport, Rhode Island, waters instead of those of the Baltic and North Sea. Although a square rig would have been more romantic, this simple marconi ketch rig, because it requires a smaller crew, is more practical.

Mirth

19'1" x 6'7" Noman's Land boat • Built by Arno Day & Joel White • Brooklin, Maine • 1959

BOTH SAILS HAVE BOOMS, which means that neither main nor mizzen sheet needs tending during a tack. But there's a gaff on the mainsail, while a sprit holds up the mizzen peak. As you can see, the gaff requires a longer mast and a throat and peak halyard; the advantage is having a bit more control over the sail's shape, and being able to lower it for reduced windage and easier furling.

Outward Bound Boat #12

29'6" x 7'11" cat ketch • Designed by Cyrus Hamlin • Built by Rittall's Boatyard • Boothbay, Maine 1971

FOR SEAWORTHINESS, YOU CAN'T BEAT A DOUBLE-ENDER—and especially one with such high ends and a smaller-than-average rig. For proof, you need only examine the record of these HIOBS (Hurricane Island Outward Bound School) double-enders. For more than 30 years, under oar and sail, they have roamed the Maine coast, Chesapeake Bay, and the Florida Keys, fair weather or foul, without serious mishap.

Twilite

15'0" x 2'6" • Designed by Gibson & Rushton • Built by Everett Smith • Canton, New York • 1974

EQUALLY ADEPT AT EITHER SAILING OR PADDLING, these decked canoes became an early American recreation vehicle for exploring rivers, lakes, and streams. This one has batwing sails, held in that shape by full-length battens. This keeps the masts short to cut down resistance when paddling upwind. Paddling or sailing, you can sit fully upright in the space just ahead of the mizzenmast.

Mist of Lemolo

30'0" x 7'9" • Designed by William Garden • Built by Bent Jespersen • Sidney, B.C., Canada • 1979

THIS BOAT AND THE THREE PRECEDING HAVE CAT KETCH RIGS, so named because there's no jib. *Mist*'s masts rotate to reef or furl the sails, so the boom goosenecks attach independently and the sails are loose-footed. The two-ply mainsail opens like the leaves of a book for sailing downwind. There are two centerboards, one forward and another aft, leaving the main cabin clear. To tack, you raise the aft board so she'll turn faster.

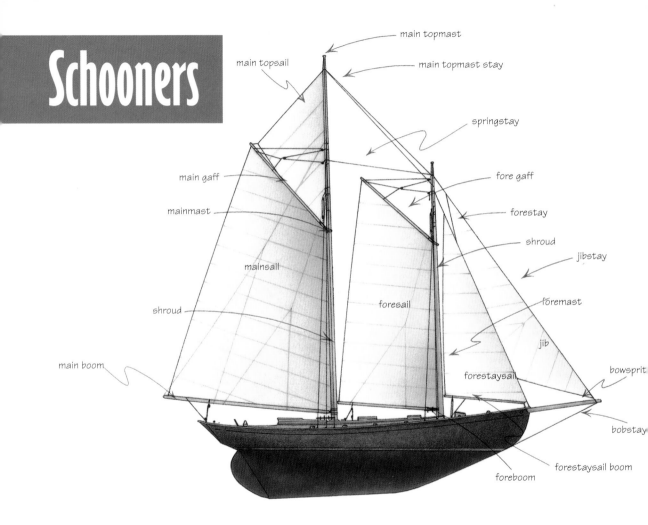

Schooners

main topmast

main topmast stay

main topsail

springstay

main gaff

fore gaff

mainmast

forestay

shroud

jibstay

mainsail

foresail

foremast

shroud

jib

main boom

forestaysail

bowsprit

bobstay

forestaysail boom

foreboom

The schooner rig, thought to have originated in America, was first used on two-masted working craft such as pinkys. Gradually, as commerce grew and vessels increased in size, wooden-hulled, cargo-carrying schooners having up to six masts and lengths of more than 300 feet were built. Schooners you're likely to see nowadays will be schooner-yachts with two masts. Along the Maine coast you'll also find a number of commercial schooners that have been converted or built new to carry passengers.

A schooner has at least two masts with a foremast that doesn't rise above the mainmast. A schooner's foresail will generally be a gaff sail, while the mainsail may be either gaff or marconi. A three-sided topsail is often set above a gaff foresail or mainsail for more speed in light winds. Small schooners may have a single headsail (a jib), while the larger ones will have two (forestaysail and jib) or three, the third usually being a jib topsail which sets on its own stay above the other two.

Gaff schooners often have fidded topmasts which extend the rig's height by means of a second mast joined to the lower mast at the doubling. So rigged, the topmast can be raised or lowered without the use of sheerlegs or the services of a crane. Staysail schooners sail to windward better than those having conventional gaff foresails. They have a mainstaysail—which is like a forestaysail but sets ahead of the mainmast—and a fisherman staysail, which is a four-sided sail that fills the remaining space between the masts.

Topsail schooners are a special (and, these days, unusual) type. They set square sails on the foretopmast above the gaff foresail. *Pride of Baltimore II* (page 138) and *Californian* (page 139) are the only examples included here. Three-masted schooners like the *Victory Chimes* (page 130) are also rare.

Summertime

52'9" x 14'0" traditional pinky • Built by George Allen • Brooklin, Maine • 1986

EARLY NEW ENGLAND FISHERMEN FAVORED THE DOUBLE-ENDED PINKY, and many were built between 1815 and 1850. Their unrivaled reputation for seaworthiness made them popular, and their utter simplicity made them affordable. No original pinky survives, but there are drawings, photographs, and models—all of which made building a replica, like *Summertime*, possible.

Mary Day

83'0" x 23'6" coaster • Designed by Capt. Havilah Hawkins, Sr. • Built by H.F. Gamage • South Bristol, Maine • 1962

BUILT FOR CARRYING PASSENGERS on weeklong coastal cruises, this schooner was originally outfitted without topmasts or jibboom—a rig not too different from *Summertime*'s. After a few years, Captain Hawkins' sons enlarged the sail plan to what you see here, greatly enhancing her light-weather performance as well as improving her looks.

Stephen Taber

68'0" x 22'5" coaster • Designed by Thomas Clapham • Built by Van Cott Shipyard • Glen Head, New York • 1871

THE OLDEST CONTINUOUSLY RIGGED CRUISE SCHOONER, the *Taber* was one of the first to switch to carrying passengers as cargo. She's a lovely little vessel, built wide and shoal as was the prevailing style, and in hull shape much like the Hudson River sloops that also claimed western Long Island Sound waters as home.

Lewis R. French

64'6" x 19'0" coaster • Modeled and built by the French Bros. • Christmas Cove, Maine • 1871

THIS COASTER WAS ALSO BUILT IN 1871, but she was shorn of her sailing rig and operated as an engine-driven cargo vessel for much of her life. Unlike the *Taber*, the *French* has no centerboard, and her hull is narrower and deeper. The resulting increase in stability allows her to carry more sails under the Coast Guard rules to which all passenger-carrying sailing vessels must comply.

Victory Chimes

132'0" x 24'0" Chesapeake Bay ram • Modeled by J.M.C. Moore • Built by George K. Phillips Co. • Bethel, Delaware • 1900

BUILT LONG AND NARROW for her work as a cargo vessel on Chesapeake Bay, the *Chimes* was also made shallow. Her narrow beam accommodated the canal width she squeaked through in passages to and from Delaware Bay. Drawing only seven feet but with full headroom under the deck, this three-master made a wonderful conversion to an ideal cruise schooner.

Nathaniel Bowditch

82'0" x 21'0" • Designed by William H. Hand, Jr. • Built by Hodgdon Bros. • East Boothbay, Maine • 1922

ONCE MORE A SCHOONER after a couple of decades as the full-powered commercial fishing dragger *Jane Dore*, the *Bowditch* makes a fitting addition to the Maine cruise schooner fleet. Whether in company or by herself, or whether she's carrying the main topsail and fisherman staysail or only the four lowers, she's always a mighty fine sight.

Mercantile

78'0" x 21'5" coaster • Modeled and built by the Billings Bros. • Little Deer Isle, Maine • 1916

SOMETIMES ENGINELESS SCHOONERS HAVE TO BE PUSHED if the wind dies, especially if night is coming on and there's an anchorage to reach before dark. Pushing is done by the diesel-driven yawlboat, which nuzzles against the schooner's stern. After the schooner anchors, the yawlboat lugs the passengers ashore to roam a nearby village or a deserted island.

Heritage

94'0" x 24'0" • Designed by Capt. Douglas K. Lee • Built by North End Shipyard • Rockland, Maine • 1983

DESIGNED FROM THE START TO CARRY PASSENGERS and to carry both a jib topsail and main topsail, *Heritage* always makes a grand sight under full sail. But, because she is so colorful as well as true to tradition, even seeing her at anchor is a real treat. She's one of a grand fleet of traditional, wooden-hulled, passenger-carrying schooners that are presently thriving. Long may their good times continue!

Alcyone

65'0" x 15'6" • Designed and built by Frank M. Prothero • Seattle, Washington • 1956

INSPIRED BY THE LINES AND RIG OF THE FAMED FISHING SCHOONERS of Massachusetts, Frank Prothero designed and built himself a smaller version in *Alcyone*. In spite of her East Coast heritage, this schooner has always called the Pacific her home waters. Her deep and stable hull allows her to carry a full complement of light-weather sails.

Spirit of Massachusetts

101'11" x 23'6" • Designed by Edw. Burgess & Melbourne Smith • Built by N. E. Historic Seaport • Boston, MA • 1984

EDWARD BURGESS MIXED YACHTING WITH FISHING in 1887 when he designed the plumb-stemmed *Carrie E. Phillips*, and in 1889 when the *Nellie Dixon* and *Fredonia* were built to another of his designs—the same one used almost a century later as the basis for the *Spirit of Massachusetts*. As the designer of three successful *America*'s Cup defenders, Burgess's association with these commercial vessels created a great deal of interest at the time.

Robertson II

105'0" x 22'0" dory fisherman • Modeled and built by W.G. McKay and Sons • Shelburne, Nova Scotia, Canada • 1940

SCHOONERS LIKE THIS CAUGHT FISH INDIRECTLY by launching two-man dories, maybe 16 of them, after reaching the fishing grounds. Each dory set a very long trawl line with baited hooks. The schooner jogged nearby, waiting for the dories to return, full of fish. Dragging (i.e., towing a net along the sea bed) subsequently replaced dory fishing and the *Robertson II* is one of the last of her type.

Adventuress

101'10" x 21'0" • Designed by B.B. Crowninshield • Built by Rice Bros. • East Boothbay, Maine • 1913

BUILT AS A YACHT, *ADVENTURESS* NOW SAILS AS A SCHOOLSHIP, teaching youngsters teamwork, community, self-worth, discipline, and other living skills through the sailing experience. Between these careers, she served as a San Francisco pilot boat for 35 years. In her present role, you're likely to find *Adventuress*, sailing or at anchor, anywhere on Puget Sound. With her rig made tall by fidded topmasts, this big schooner can be easily spotted.

Pride of Baltimore II

96'6" x 26'6" Baltimore clipper • Designed by Thomas C. Gillmer • Built by G. Peter Boudreau • Baltimore, MD • 1988

DISTINGUISHABLE BY HER RAKISH RIG, this replica vessel replaces an earlier *Pride* that capsized and sunk in a freak squall. This vessel is larger and better able to withstand high winds in spite of her large sail plan. Her loose-footed foresail and the squaresails set above it demand unusually fine seamanship—which is just what she gets. She's not a passenger-carrying vessel, but rather a kind of wide-ranging ambassador for the state of Maryland.

Californian

93'6" x 24'6" revenue cutter replica • Designed and built by Melbourne Smith • San Diego, California • 1983

FAST AND WEATHERLY, topsail schooners patrolled the coast in the days of sail for the U.S. Revenue Marine— forerunner of the Coast Guard. *Californian* is a recently built replica and, like her predecessors, is an unusually fine sailer. Although she's at sea much of the time along the western coastline from Mexico to Canada, her mission now is quite different. As California's official tall ship, she's a roving ambassador and a schoolship.

Silver Heels

41'2" x 12'0" • Designed by Murray G. Peterson • Built by Camden Shipbuilding Co. • Camden, Maine • 1963

A PETERSON SCHOONER IS WIDELY ADMIRED—so much so that it has become a recognizable type, much like a Friendship sloop or a Cape Cod catboat. It all began around 1930 with the three beautifully detailed schooners named *Coaster* that Murray Peterson designed and had built for himself. But perhaps the best of the breed are *Silver Heels* and her two near-sisters built in the 1960s under Malcolm Brewer's supervision.

Defiance

45'0" x 13'10" • Designed by Murray G. Peterson • Built by Paul E. Luke • East Boothbay, Maine • 1960

SHE FLOATS IN ONLY 4½ FEET OF WATER with the centerboard raised, opening up more cruising options than a boat with a deeper draft. The owner was well aware of this advantage when she had *Defiance* designed and built because her previous boat was also a shallow keel/centerboarder. Beautiful sails enhance a beautiful boat, and in this regard, *Defiance*'s sails excel on at least two counts: the narrow panels and the off-white color.

Brigadoon

49'11" x 13'2" • Designed by L. Francis Herreshoff • Built by Britt Bros. • West Lynn, Massachusetts • 1924

CLIPPER BOWS BECAME THIS DESIGNER'S SPECIALTY, showing up in several of his enduring designs like *Ticonderoga* (page 104) and *Araminta* (page 111). But *Brigadoon*'s clipper bow was his first. Launched as the baldheaded schooner *Joann*, her appearance was much improved when actor Sterling Hayden bought her and gave her a larger, more traditional rig with a main topmast.

Spike Africa

61'4" x 15'7" • Designed and built by Robert Sloan • Costa Mesa, California • 1977

A LONGTIME FAN OF PETERSON SCHOONERS, Bob Sloan designed *Spike* with a cargo hold and installed a big engine so he could use her commercially. Together, Sloan and his schooner ranged all along the West Coast from Mexico to Alaska, and across the Pacific to Hawaii and back, with cargo or as a towboat with one or more sailboats astern. More recently, chartering has become *Spike*'s stock in trade.

Elizabeth Muir

48'0" x 11'7" • Designed by Eldredge-McInnis • Built by Lamerdin & Linderman • Bolinas, California • 1991

HER DESIGN DATES FROM THE 1930S and came from an office known mostly for its powerboats. Because the design's hull shape is so well thought out, not only in its original gaff schooner configuration, but as a cutter and as the staysail schooner rig shown here, it's likely that Walter McInnis could have become as well-known as, say, John Alden, had he focused more on sail and less on power.

Malabar II

41'2" x 11'2" • Designed by John G. Alden • Built by Charles A. Morse & Son • Thomaston, Maine • 1922

CHARMING IN HER SIMPLICITY, *Malabar II* looks as natural as the wooded shoreline she's passing. Without the distraction of glitter or shine, your eye goes to the graceful proportions. Gaff schooners go best when the sheets can be eased like this, on a beam reach. For driving to windward, it's not the ideal rig—but with forethought, most closehauled sailing can be avoided.

Voyager

50'0" x 14'0" • Designed by John G. Alden • Built by Charles A. Morse & Son • Thomaston, Maine • 1929

IT TAKES ONLY A SMALL CREW TO SAIL A SCHOONER *VOYAGER*'S SIZE. Her husband-and-wife owners made passage after passage alone during this schooner's circumnavigation. She's sailing here off the coast of Moorea in the South Pacific. Living up to her name, *Voyager* already had a lot of miles under her keel before beginning the odyssey. And with the sensible care she receives, there are thousands of miles yet to come.

When and If

63'5" x 15'1" • Designed by John G. Alden • Built by F. F. Pendleton • Wiscasset, Maine • 1939

MARCONI MAINSAILS IMPROVE ON-THE-WIND PERFORMANCE because they have more forward drive than a gaff sail of equal area. As you can see, both of *When and If*'s masts are proportionally taller than *Voyager*'s, allowing for a third headsail and, between the masts, a fisherman staysail. These boost her speed in light air, but add complexity. Trade-offs like this are often called for in designing a rig—or an entire boat, for that matter.

Spirit

47'0" x 12'0" • Designed by John G. Alden • Built by Hodgdon Bros. • East Boothbay, Maine • 1934

JOHN ALDEN ROSE TO FAME THROUGH HIS BEAUTIFUL SCHOONER DESIGNS, but their era was coming to a close when this one, launched as *Discovery III*, was designed. Alden's early *Malabars* (there were 10 schooners of that name) were consistent race winners, but by the mid-1930s marconi yawls proved themselves superior and schooners went out of favor—at least for racing.

Rainbird

40'6" x 10'2" • Designed and built by William Garden • Seattle, Washington • 1949

A KNOCKABOUT-STYLE GRAND BANKS FISHING SCHOONER IN MINIATURE, *Rainbird* has the same long, lean bow and narrow, heart-shaped transom. But the tall mainmast departs from tradition, its purpose being to help spread more sail. Puget Sound is *Rainbird*'s home, where the wind is gentle. A genoa helps light-air performance too, and the pilothouse befits the schooner's name as it shelters the crew from inclement weather.

Mya

49'10" x 12'1" • Designed by Concordia Co. • Built by Duxbury Boat Yard • Duxbury, Massachusetts • 1940

HER DESIGN FOLLOWED THE CONCORDIA YAWL, and it's easy to spot the family resemblance: a lovely sheerline, generous overhangs, freeboard on the low side. She's slimmer and sleeker than most schooners, and has proven very fast. *Mya* now sports a blue hull under her present owner, and you'll most likely see her in the waters just south of Cape Cod.

Brilliant

61'6" x 14'8" • Designed by Sparkman & Stephens, Inc. • Built by Henry B. Nevins, Inc. • City Island, New York • 1932

COST WAS NO OBJECT when *Brilliant* was ordered; the owner wanted only a seakindly hull of great strength and the best materials and workmanship. Quality construction and consistent good care have kept *Brilliant*'s teak topsides flawless and her hull sound. Her tall foremast enables a good-sized headsail to be set, which contributes to this schooner's reputation for speed.

Astor

73'0" x 15'4"• Designed by W. & R.B. Fife • Built by W. Fife & Son • Fairlie, Scotland • 1924

RERIGGED AS A STAYSAIL SCHOONER with significantly less sail area than originally designed, *Astor* is no slouch. Sails on stays pull more than those attached to masts, when sailing closehauled, because their leading edges are in clear air rather than eddies. That's why the staysail schooner became a favorite—especially for 'round-the-buoy racing where a good deal of the sailing is to windward.

Fortune

50'8" x 9'8" • Designed by B.B. Crowninshield • Built by Crowninshield Shipbldg. Co. • So. Somerset, MA • 1925

***FORTUNE* DOESN'T SEEM TO KNOW SHE'S A SCHOONER** when she's jammed hard on the wind. She goes to windward like a sloop, but enjoys the lower rating of a schooner, making her a consistent winner. She's very slimlined, and this, of course, makes her slippery as well. Her owner realizes it takes good sails to go fast, and *Fortune* always has the best.

Vintage

45'0" x 15'0" scow schooner • Designed by R.D. Culler • Built by Brooklin Boat Yard • Brooklin, Maine • 1986

A LOT OF BOAT FOR HER LENGTH because of her pram-type bow, shallow draft is another of this schooner's virtues. She's a heavily built centerboarder with lots of initial stability, so her deck stays relatively level, making it easy to walk around. Her weight gives her an easy motion as well. An engine, running only a little above an idle, greatly enhances her windward ability.

Ellen

36'0" x 11'6" pinky • Designed by Chapelle & Porter • Built by Stephen Slauenwhite • Mader's Cove, N. S., Canada • 1980

THERE'S A CHALLENGE IN NOT HAVING AN ENGINE, and meeting that challenge can bring real satisfaction. That was exactly what *Ellen*'s owner had in mind. An engineless boat not only requires good seamanship, but patience as well—for those times when there's no wind. *Ellen*'s fine-lined hull, while traditional for Down East pinkys, allows her to sail more spritely than full-bodied, Massachusetts-type pinkys like *Summertime*.

Glossary

abeam Alongside; roughly 90 degrees from a vessel's heading.

aft, abaft Toward the stern.

backstay Standing rigging that leads aft and holds a mast from bending forward and perhaps breaking. A backstay also serves to keep an opposing headstay tight. *See* running backstays.

ballast keel The iron or lead casting attached to the lower part of the hull along its centerline that provides stability to a sailing craft.

batten A long, thin, somewhat flexible piece of hardwood or plastic that inserts in a pocket sewn into the leech of a sail to keep it from curling. Battens allow the leech to be convex. *See* roach.

beam reach A point of sailing on which the wind comes from abeam.

bitts Vertical posts for securing docklines, towlines, anchor rodes, or pieces of running rigging.

block A pulley having a sheave, a shell, and some type of end connection through which a line can pass to change its direction or, in combination with other blocks, to provide a mechanical advantage—as in a block and tackle.

boom The spar that runs along the foot, or lower edge, of a sail.

boomkin A fixed, horizontal spar that projects aft beyond the hull for attaching the backstay and often the mizzen sheet of a yawl or ketch or the main sheet of a sloop or cutter.

bow The forward end of a boat's hull.

bowsprit A fixed, horizontal spar that projects beyond the bow having one or more headstays attached at the outboard end.

cat *See* chapter introduction, page 9.

catboat A shallow-bodied, wide sailboat that carries a cat rig. Usually decked and sometimes has a cabin; catboats generally have origins in Cape Cod, Great South Bay, or Barnegat Bay.

centerboard A wood or metal panel, contained in a watertight trunk or case, that can be lowered through a slot in a boat's bottom and whose purpose is to prevent leeway. Centerboards pivot on a transverse pin at their forward, lower corner and are hoisted by a rod or pennant attached near their after, top corner.

clew The aft, lower corner of a fore-and-aft sail; one of the two lower corners of a squaresail.

clipper bow A bow that is concave in profile and usually terminates with a decorative carving known as a billethead. These bows are often further adorned with trailboards that extend aft along the sheer from the billethead.

coaming The projecting rim around a cockpit or other low deck structure.

cockpit The sunken space from which the helmsman steers the boat with wheel or tiller and where the passengers usually congregate.

cutter *See* chapter introduction, page 59.

davits Stationary or swinging arms used for hoisting a small boat, such as a yawlboat, out of the water. Also used singly for lifting other items such as anchors.

deckhouse An enclosure, with windows, built rela-tively high above the deck, that provides some degree of shelter. Deckhouses are likely to open aft into the cockpit.

double-ender A boat, yacht, or vessel that is pointed at both ends.

fairlead A device through which a line passes to change its direction.

felucca A sailing workboat of Italian origin that is double-ended, partly decked, and has lateen sails.

fisherman staysail A four-sided, light-weather sail that is hoisted between the masts of a schooner to fill the space above a gaff foresail.

flush deck A deck without a trunk cabin; usually found only on larger yachts.

foot The lower edge of a sail.

foremast The forwardmost mast of a schooner.

forestay As opposed to a backstay, standing rigging that leads forward and holds the mast from bending aft and perhaps breaking, and to which a jib or forestaysail may be attached. If there are other stays performing the same service, the forestay is usually the lowest and farthest inboard.

forestaysail If more than one headsail, a three-sided jib-type sail, attached to the forestay, that often has a boom along its foot.

fractional rig A rig in which the jibstay terminates partway down the mast, as opposed to a masthead rig where the stay attaches all the way at the top.

Friendship sloop A clipper-bowed, gaff-rigged sloop with a raking, elliptical transom originally used for lobstering in midcoast Maine, and nowadays used for pleasure. Many were built in the town of Friendship.

gaff The spar to which the head of a gaff sail is attached. Gaffs and their sails are raised and lowered by halyards, usually a throat halyard at the forward end, and a peak halyard farther aft.

gaff rig A sailing rig that carries a gaff sail.

gaff sail A four-sided sail the head of which attaches to a gaff and the luff of which attaches to a mast.

gallows frame An archlike structure that supports the outboard end of a boom when the sail is lowered.

genoa A big, usually low-cut headsail that overlaps the mast outside the shrouds.

gooseneck The fitting that attaches a boom to a mast.

gunter A sail with a spar attached to the upper part of its luff that, when hoisted, stands nearly vertical and becomes, in effect, an extension of the mast and gives the appearance of being a marconi sail.

handicapping formula A time allowance formula that takes such measurements as length, beam, and sail area into account so that boats of unequal size and design can compete on equal terms in the same race.

head The upper corner of a triangular sail; the upper edge of a four-sided sail.

headsail Any sail, usually three-sided, that is attached to a stay forward of the forwardmost mast.

headstay The uppermost stay forward of the mast; usually found on a yacht with a double head rig.

helm A tiller or wheel used to steer the boat.

jib A headsail, smaller than a genoa, attached to the forestay or jibstay.

jibboom The spar, sometimes called a jib club, attached to the foot (lower edge) of a jib; also, a spar that attaches to and extends beyond a bowsprit.

jibstay Another word for forestay in a boat carrying single headsails; also, the forwardmost stay of boats with double headsails.

jiffy reefing A rigging arrangement for shortening a sail consisting of a metal hook at the gooseneck which engages a reef cringle in the sail's luff, and an outhaul pennant opposite, by which the leech of the sail can be pulled downward and outward so the sail is snugged to the boom in a reefed condition.

ketch *See* chapter introduction, page 103.

knockabout A sloop-rigged day boat, usually having a small cabin and no bowsprit; may have a full keel or keel/centerboard combination; also, a style of bow profile having considerable overhang and a convex shape as opposed to the concave shape of a clipper bow.

lateen A three-sided sail with a spar along its upper (and longest) edge that is hoisted on a short mast to about 45 degrees. A felucca's sail is an example.

leech The aft edge of a sail.

leeward Away or farther from the wind, as one boat may be to leeward of another; or the side of a boat that is away from the wind.

loose-footed A sail that is attached to the boom only at its lower corners, or one having no boom at all.

lugsail A four-sided sail permanently attached to a spar along its top (head) edge, which in turn is hoisted by a single halyard so that approximately one-quarter of its length projects forward of the mast.

luff The forward edge of a sail. As a verb, to head into the wind so the sail is flapping.

mainsail A sail with its luff (forward edge) attached to the mainmast, usually by means of hoops or slides.

marconi rig A rig in which the mainsail is three-sided and comes nearly to a point at its head.

masthead rig A rig in which the forestay terminates at the masthead.

mizzen mast The aftermost mast of a ketch, yawl, or three-masted schooner.

outhaul Mechanism at the outboard end of the boom for adjusting tension along the foot of the sail.

peak The aft, top corner of a gaff sail.

pinky A full-bodied, schooner-rigged double-ender whose bulwarks extend beyond the upper part of the rudder and terminate in a small, dorylike transom.

rake An aftward or (less frequently) a forward slant from vertical.

rating The numerical result of a handicapping formula.

reef To reduce sail area by partly lowering a sail and gathering and securing its foot.

reeve To thread a line through a block or other fairlead-type opening.

rig The combination of mast(s), boom(s), standing and running rigging, and sails that propel a sailing craft.

roach The portion of a sail that lies beyond a straight line connecting its head or peak and its clew. Roach can be positive as in a mainsail whose leech is convex, or negative as in a genoa's concave leech.

rod rigging Standing rigging made from solid rod rather than stranded wire.

rove Past tense of *reeve.*

rudder The flat blade that swings from side to side underwater and is used to steer the boat.

running rigging The halyards, sheets, topping lifts, and other cordage used to operate and control a boat's rig.

running backstays Pairs of adjustable stays used to hold the mast from bending forward and possibly breaking. In use, the windward runner is kept tight while the leeward one has to be slacked so as not to interfere with the sail or boom. Running backstays must be tended when tacking.

schooner *See* chapter introduction, page 125.

sheer The curve of the edge of the deck or rail as viewed in profile or plan.

sheerlegs An A-frame structure for hoisting heavy weights.

sheet A line used to adjust a sail after it has been raised. Sheets may be attached directly to the clew of a sail (as on a headsail), or to a boom.

shrouds The standing rigging that holds a mast against transverse forces. They are usually made of wire and can be adjusted at their lower ends by means of turnbuckles.

skipjack A type of sloop-rigged workboat with a V-bottom hull, a raking mast, and a bowsprit used for oystering on Chesapeake Bay.

sloop *See* chapter introduction, page 23.

spidsgatter A small, double-ended cruising sloop of Danish origin.

spinnaker A three-sided, parachutelike sail used to increase a boat's sail area when sailing downwind. A spinnaker is attached only at its three corners by a halyard, a sheet, and a guy.

spitfire jib A small, rugged headsail; a storm jib.

spliced-eye standing rigging Shrouds and stays whose upper ends terminate in spliced loops around the mast.

spreader A relatively short and level strut that projects athwartships from each side of a mast partway up, over which shrouds pass.

sprit A relatively light, diagonally-oriented spar that holds up the peak of a spritsail.

standing rigging The wires, such as shrouds and stays, that support a mast.

staysail A sail whose luff is attached to the forestay or, in a staysail schooner, to the mainstay between the fore and mainmasts. Also a light-weather sail set forward of a ketch's or yawl's mizzenmast.

stern The aft end of a boat's hull.

storm trysail A small, very ruggedly built, three-sided sail that can be set in lieu of the mainsail when the wind is very strong.

tabloid cruiser A small sailboat, usually under 25 feet, with a shelter cabin, a Spartan galley, and berths (usually two) for sleeping.

tack The forward, lower corner of a sail. As a verb, to change direction about 90 degrees, through the eye of the wind, so the sails fill on the opposite side. A port tack is when the wind blows across the boat from port to starboard; a starboard tack is the opposite.

throat The forward, top corner of a gaff sail.

tiller A (usually) curved and tapered stick that connects to the rudderstock and is used for steering the boat.

topmast An extention of the lower mast suitable for carrying a topsail; can be either a separate spar joined at the doubling, or a continuation of the lower mast.

topsail A three-sided sail that sets above a gaff and fills the area between the topmast and the gaff; a four-sided sail whose head (upper edge) attaches to the yard of a topsail schooner.

transom The flat or curved panel that encloses the after end of the hull.

trunk cabin A low boxlike structure built up from the deck to provide more headroom. Trunk cab-

ins usually have portholes or windows in their sides to let in light and fresh air, and may have raised aft portions called doghouses.

turnbuckles Threaded, adjustable metal fittings attaching shrouds and stays to the hull or deck.

weathercock The tendency of a boat's bow to head into the wind as in a yawl whose mizzen is tightly sheeted.

weather helm The pull the helmsman must exert on the tiller or wheel to hold a steady course against the boat's natural tendency to head into the wind.

whisker pole A light spar used for pushing out the clew of a headsail when sailing downwind.

windward Toward or closer to the wind, as one boat may be to windward of another; also, the side of a boat that the wind hits first.

yankee A three-sided, high-cut headsail whose luff is attached to the headstay and usually used in combination with a forestaysail.

yard The spar to which the head of a squaresail, lugsail, or lateen sail is attached.

yawl *See* chapter introduction, page 77.

yawlboat A small, open, engine-driven boat that services an unpowered sailing vessel. When not in use, yawlboats are often hoisted on the big vessel's stern davits so as to be clear of the water.

Index

Buzzards Bay 12½: *Quisset*, 36
Buzzards Bay 25: *Naiad*, 29
Californian, 139
Camden Shipbuilding Co.: *Silver Heels*, 140
Camper & Nicholson, Ltd.: *Astra*, 51
Campos, Manuel: *Vito Dumas*, 61
Cantieri Baglietto: *Tioga*, 92
Cape Cod catboat: *Breck Marshall*, 12; *Cimba*, 10; *Conjurer*, 11
Cat: Andros Dinghy, 20; Beetle Cat, 14; *Breck Marshall*, 12; *Cimba*, 10; *Conjurer*, 11; *Finch*, 16; *Hesperus*, 21; *Josef W.*, 15; *Mary Ann*, 19; Nutshell Prams, 17; *Peggotty*, 13; *Silent Maid*, 18; *Windrose*, 21
Chadwick, James: *Eastward*, 26
Chapelle, H. I.: *Ellen*, 155; *Summertime*, 126
Chautauqua, 108
Chips, 31
Cimba, 10
Circe, 34
Cirrus, 82
Clapham, Thomas: *Stephen Taber*, 128
Clover, 45
Concordia Co.: Beetle Cat, 14; *Free Spirit*, 44; *Mya*, 150; *Naiad*, 29; *Starlight*, 100

Concordia 33: *Free Spirit*, 44
Concordia yawl: *Starlight*, 100
Conjurer, 11
Cookson, Harry: *Freda*, 24
Crane, Clinton H.: *Gleam*, 50
Crocker, S. S.: *Chautauqua*, 108; *Jarges Pride*, 62; *Lands End*, 109
Crosby Yacht Building: *Conjurer*, 11; *Owl*, 33
Crosby, Charles: *Breck Marshall*, 12
Crosby, H. Manley: *Conjurer*, 11; *Owl*, 33
Crowninshield. B.B.: *Adventuress*, 137; *Fortune*, 153; *Quill II*
Culler, R.D.: *Vintage*, 154
Curlew, 38
Customary Boats: *Curlew*, 38
Cutter: *Able*, 60; *Anne Marie II*, 71; *Arawak*, 69; *Baccarat*, 63; *Bryony*, 70; *Hirta*, 75; *Jarges Pride*, 62; *Lizzie Annie*, 74; *Masuyo*, 72; *Mimi Rose*, 67; *Morning Star*, 73; *Northern Crown*, 64; *Shiris*, 68; *Skye*, 66; *Sweet Olive*, 65; *Vito Dumas*, 61
Cutts & Case: *Rebellion*, 46
Cutts, Edmund: *Rebellion*, 46
Day, Arno: *Mirth*, 120
Defiance, 141
Delaware ducker: *Josef W.*, 15

Derecktor, Robert E.: *Clover*, 45
Desperate Lark, 84
Dickie, A.M. & Sons: *Moonshine*, 113
Dolphin, 41
Dorade, 80
Dow, Eric: *Shimmer*, 37
Dram, 49
Duxbury Boat Yard: *Mya*, 150
Dyon, 30
Eastern Shipbuilding Corp.: *Arawak*, 69
Eastward, 26
Edna E. Lockwood, 118
Eio, 42
Eldredge-McInnis: *Elizabeth Muir*, 144
Elfitz, 32
Elizabeth Muir, 144
Ellen, 155
Eppick, William & Elaine: *Skye*, 66
Escapade, 99
Felucca: *Nuovo Mondo*, 56
Ferguson, R.: *Free Spirit*, 44
Fife, W. & R. B.: *Astor*, 152; *Hallowe'en*, 98
Fife, William, III: *Sumurun*, 106
Fife, Wm. & Son: *Astor*, 152; *Belle Aventure*, 107; *Hallowe'en*, 98; *Sumurun*, 106
Finch, 16

About the Photographer and Author

Benjamin Mendlowitz has devoted his professional life to capturing the magic of wooden boats in color photography. His annual *Calendar of Wooden Boats* has won awards for photography and design. His work has regularly appeared in feature articles and on the covers of the most respected magazines in the boating field as well as in many general interest magazines and books. A one-man show of his photographs has been exhibited at maritime museums around the country since it opened at the Philadelphia Maritime Museum. Previous books of his color photographs of wooden boats include *Wood, Water & Light*, *A Passage in Time*, and *The Book of Wooden Boats*. He lives in Brooklin, Maine.

Maynard Bray has been building, restoring, and writing about boats most of his life. After 13 years as a marine engineer he became shipyard supervisor at Mystic Seaport where he directed the restoration and enlargement of the museum's watercraft collection, the construction of the shipyard, and the refloating of the whaleship *Charles W. Morgan*. In 1975 he moved to Brooklin, Maine, and in 1979 became *Wooden Boat* magazine's technical editor. Still a contributing editor and Brooklin resident, he continues to supervise the restoration of fine wooden yachts and to write prolifically about boats in books and articles. His books include *Mystic Seaport Watercraft* and (as co-author) *Herreshoff of Bristol*. He has provided the text for the *Calendar of Wooden Boats* for 15 years.